LIES

FULL OF IT

BEST LIAR

**ONLY AND ONLY TO BEST LIAR. YUP!
THATS ME...**

Contents

Prologue

LIES LIES LIES JUST LIES.

Foreword

AGAIN LIES LIES AND MORE LIES.

Acknowledgements

WHAT DO YOU THINK NOW?

ITS THE SAME LIES LIES LIES LIES...

Preface

YOU STILL HERE?

OK THEN!

LETS GOOOOOO!

FIND THE ONLY "TRUTH" IN THESE SO MANY LIES.

THAT THE RARITY OF TRUTH IN THIS WORLD!

don't just mark it in the heading genius! (find it down)

LIES LIES LIES LIES LIES LIES LIES LIES LIES LIES LIES LIES LIES LIES LIES LIES LIES LIES LIES LIES LIESLIES LIES LIES LIES LIES LIES LIES LIES LIES LIES LIES LIES LIES LIES LIES LIES LIES LIES LIES LIES LIES LIES LIES LIES LIES LIES LIES LIES LIES LIES LIES LIES LIES LIES LIES LIES LIES LIES LIES LIES LIES LIES LIES

LIES LIES LIES LIES LIES LIES LIES LIES
LIES LIES LIES LIES LIES LIES LIES LIES
LIES LIES LIES LIES LIES LIES LIES LIES
LIES LIES LIES LIES LIES LIES LIES LIES
LIES LIES LIES LIES LIES LIES LIES LIES
LIES LIES LIES LIES LIES LIES LIES LIES
LIES LIES LIES LIES LIES LIES LIES LIES
LIES LIES LIES LIES LIES LIES LIES LIES
LIES LIES LIES LIES LIES LIES LIES LIES
LIES LIES LIES LIES LIES LIES LIES LIES
LIES LIES LIES LIES LIES LIES LIES LIES
LIES LIES LIES LIES LIES LIES LIES LIES
LIES LIES LIES LIES LIES LIES LIES LIES
LIES LIES LIES LIES LIES LIES LIES LIES
LIES LIES LIES LIES LIES LIES LIES LIES
LIES LIES LIES LIES LIES LIES LIES LIES
LIES LIES LIES LIES LIES LIES LIES LIES
LIES LIES LIES LIES LIES LIES LIES LIES
LIES LIES LIES LIES LIES LIES LIES LIES
LIES LIES LIES LIES LIES LIES LIES LIES
LIES LIES LIES LIES LIES LIES LIES LIES
LIES LIES LIES TRUTH LIES LIES LIES LIES
LIES LIES LIES LIES LIES LIES LIES LIES
LIES LIES LIES LIES LIES LIES LIES LIES
LIES LIES LIES LIES LIES LIES LIES LIES
LIES LIES LIES LIES LIES LIES LIES LIES
LIES LIES LIES LIES LIES LIES LIES LIES
LIES LIES LIES LIES LIES LIES LIES LIES
LIES LIES LIES LIES LIES LIES LIES LIES
LIES LIES LIES LIES LIES LIES LIES LIES
LIES LIES LIES LIES LIES LIES LIES LIES
LIES LIES LIES LIES LIES LIES LIES LIES
LIES LIES LIES LIES LIES LIES LIES LIES

LIES LIES LIES LIES LIES LIES LIES LIES
LIES LIES LIES LIES LIES LIES LIES LIES
LIES LIES LIES LIES LIES LIES LIES LIES
LIES LIES LIES LIES LIES LIES LIES LIES
LIES LIES LIES LIES LIES LIES LIES LIES
LIES LIES LIES LIES LIES LIES LIES LIES
LIES LIES LIES LIES LIES LIES LIES LIES
LIES LIES LIES LIES LIES LIES LIES LIES
LIES LIES LIES LIES LIES LIES LIES LIES
LIES LIES LIES LIES LIES LIES LIES LIES
LIES LIES LIES LIES LIES LIES LIES LIES
LIES LIES LIES LIES LIES LIES LIES LIES
LIES LIES LIES LIES LIES LIES LIES LIES
LIES LIES LIES LIES LIES LIES LIES LIES
LIES LIES LIES LIES LIES LIES LIES LIES
LIES LIES LIES LIES LIES LIES LIES LIES
LIES LIES LIES LIES LIES LIES LIES LIES
LIES LIES LIES LIES LIES LIES LIES LIES
LIES LIES LIES LIES LIES LIES LIES LIES
LIES LIES LIES LIES LIES LIES LIES LIES
LIES LIES LIES LIES LIES LIES LIES LIES
LIES LIES LIES LIES LIES LIES LIES LIES
LIES LIES LIES LIES LIES LIES LIES LIES
LIES LIES LIES LIES LIES LIES LIES LIES
LIES LIES LIES LIES LIES LIES LIES LIES
LIES LIES LIES LIES LIES LIES LIES LIES
LIES LIES LIES LIES LIES LIES LIES LIES
LIES LIES LIES LIES LIES LIES LIES LIES
LIES LIES LIES LIES LIES LIES LIES LIES
LIES LIES LIES LIES LIES LIES LIES LIES
LIES LIES LIES LIES LIES LIES LIES LIES
LIES LIES LIES LIES LIES LIES LIES LIES
LIES LIES LIES LIES LIES LIES LIES LIES

LIES LIES...

CHAPTER ONE

NO CHAPTERS DUDE

1. Napoléon Was Short

A tall tale. At 1.68m, he was slightly above average height for a Frenchman of the time.

2. Don't Eat and Swim

This doesn't increase the risk of cramps; alcohol is the biggest risk increaser.

3. Salted Water Boils Quicker

Adding a sprinkle of salt to fresh water makes no noticeable difference.

4. Oil Stops Stuck Pasta

It doesn't prevent sticking. But it can stop the water boiling over.

5. Left and Right Brain

There's no solid division between hemispheres; the left brain can learn "right- brain skills" and vice versa.

6. Dropped Coins from a Tall Building Kill

The terminal velocity of a penny is 48-80km/h. Not fast enough to kill – but it sure would sting.

7. Three Wise Men

Nowhere in the Bible does it specify that there were three.

8. MSG = Headaches

There's no scientific proof – just anecdotal evidence implicating monosodium glutamate.

9. Dogs Sweat by Salivating

No – they regulate temperature through panting. They actually sweat through their footpads.

10. Great Wall of China

It's not visible from space. No single human structure is visible from orbit, but you can see cities at night.

11. Flush Rotation

A flushed toilet doesn't drain the other way in the opposite hemisphere. The Coriolis effect doesn't apply to water in toilets.

12. Einstein Failed Maths

No. He failed an entrance exam for a school, two years early, but still excelled in maths.

13. Humans and Dinosaurs

Despite 41% of US adults thinking we coexisted, we actually missed each other by 64 million years.

14. Black Holes Absorb Everything

Not really "holes", but rather hugely dense objects with massive gravitational pull.

15. We Have Only 5 Senses

Many scientists insist on 21, including balance, pain, movement, hunger, thirst, etc.

16. Vaccines Cause Autism

Groundless fears based on fraudulent research that's been shown to have been manipulated.

17. Don't Touch Baby Birds

Most birds have a limited sense of smell, so they won't abandon babies who "smell" of humans.

18. Alcohol Kills Brain Cells

While rampant alcohol use can damage the brain, it's not due to cell death.

19. Missing-Persons Reports

You don't have to wait 24 hours to report someone as missing to the police if you have serious concerns about their safety.

20. Different Tongue Parts

There are not different sections of the tongue for each taste: bitter, sour, salty, sweet, and umami (savoury/meaty).

21. Only 10% of the Brain is Used

Metaphor that's been misunderstood; not all neurons are always firing, but inactive cells are still important.

22. Iron Maidens

These were never medieval torture devices, but 18th-century fakes were created for sensational circuses.

23. Body Heat and the Head

Only in infants is most heat lost through the head (unless the head is the only uncovered part of the body).

24. Wake Sleepwalkers?

They'll be really confused, but it's OK. They're more likely to hurt themselves if they're not awoken.

25. Bananas Grow on Trees

Actually, they grow on massive herbs that just resemble trees.

26. Milk Increases Mucus

Nope; it doesn't. There's no need to avoid dairy if you have a cold.

27. Bats Are Blind

Not only can bats see, but they also use echolocation. That's why they're so awesome!

28. Caffeine Dehydrates You

Not really. The diuretic effect of caffeine is offset by the amount of water in a caffeinated drink.

29. Goldfish's 3-Second Memory

While not the smartest in the animal kingdom, goldfish do boast a better memory than most politicians.

30. Shaving Thickens Hair

Regrown hair isn't thicker, coarser, or darker; it just appears so because it grows back with a blunt tip.

31. Seven Years to Digest Gum

The chewy base of gum is indigestible and passes straight through. The remainder is absorbed.

32. Vikings' Horns

The helmets were created by a costume designer for a 19th- century Wagner opera.

33. Alcohol Keeps You Warm

It merely dilates warm blood vessels near the skin, creating the impression of warmth. It can actually drop core body temperature.

34. The Vomitorium

Not a room Romans used for Bacchanalian binges, but the name for the entrance to a stadium.

35. Sugar = Hyperactivity

Studies have disproved this. Poor or rowdy behaviours still occur in children with sugar-free diets.

36. Bulls Hate Red

Bulls are colour-blind. They actually perceive the motions of the bullfighter's cloth as a threat.

CHAPTER TWO

HAHA! CHAPTER

This may not have hit your radar when it happened, and even if it did, you may not have considered it a second time. But we did it, my friend, we did it. In 2005, the Spitzer Space Telescope (launched in 2003) produced convincing evidence that the Milky Way is not the simplest galaxy you have ever seen reflecting your life. It is a real orbiting galaxy. So instead of the luxurious arms protruding from the center, there is a large fat bar in the center, and the arms of our galaxy sprout from both ends.

Now, scientists have been debating this and have been trying to come up with incredible evidence for some time. And when they did - not much happened. Some mainstream news outlets have given it little time to broadcast, and the astronomical community discussed it for a while. When all the devotees in the universe knew about it, all the others went on in a state of bliss, not realizing that they were thinking of the galaxy in which they lived all that was wrong.

From geography to physiology, there are many examples of people who collectively do wrong by reading a myth as a fact. Here are 10 of the biggest mistakes you make in making known facts.

10: Mount Everest Is The Tallest Mountain in the World

Mount Everest is one whopping big mountain, but is it the tallest in the world? In fact it is not. A mountain is highest in regard to how far it soars above sea level. But technically it is tallest from base to summit. And Mauna Kea kills it at being the tallest.

Here's the deets: Above sea level, Mauna Kea (in Hawaii) is only 13,799 feet (4,206 meters). But when you count the crazy enormous portion of it that's underwater, it's 33,465 feet tall (10,200 meters). Everest, that snobby little upstart, is only 29,029 feet (8,848 meters) above sea level, with none of it below sea level [source: Mitchinson and Lloyd].

But the shame doesn't end there. Mount Kilimanjaro hasn't taken the stand yet. Kilimanjaro is 19,340 feet (5,895 meters) top to bottom. So it's not as tall as Everest – but Everest is surrounded by the rest of its friends, the Himalayas, all of which are collectively growing by a quarter of an inch per year and pushing Everest's summit higher. Kilimanjaro, on the other hand, is solitary, rising out from the relative flatness of Tanzania all on its dramatically striking own [source: Mitchinson and Lloyd].

9: Body Heat Dissipates Mainly Through the Head

Look at my cool hat! It is keeping my head warm. Sort of like my clothes are keeping my rest of me warm.

You lose most of your body heat through your head because there are so many blood vessels in your scalp. Or because there's not a lot of fat between your scalp and your skull. Or because there's a lot of circulation keeping your brain warm. Or something. At least, that's what we've all heard. That's why you need to wear a hat in the winter: Otherwise you'll catch cold.

But, the sad truth is, you lose just as much heat per square inch through your head as you do through the rest of the body, a fact that would become abundantly clear if you ever tried to scrape the frost off your windshield while naked. (We don't recommend trying that experiment.)

So if you're out on a wintry day and you notice that your head seems to be particularly cold compared to the rest of your body, it's probably because your head is bare, and everything else is sensibly bundled up. Putting on a hat will fix that problem.

It's less likely to keep you from catching a cold, though.

8: The Great Wall of China Is the Only Man-made Object Visible From Space

The Great Wall of China gets a double whammy on this myth. You can see other man-made objects from space (especially when the part of the Earth being viewed is awash in the artificially illuminated glow of nighttime). It's also pretty hard to pick out the Great Wall of China from any space-based locale. In low-Earth orbit, it's next to impossible to see it with the naked eye. Even with a fairly hefty camera lens, it's still challenging to tell if you're looking at the Great Wall or not.

There are a couple of reasons this pseudo-fact is so far-flung. For one, its history dates back to well before the Space Age, so no one knew enough to nip it in the bud straight off. And for another, the Great Wall of China is, well, a giant wall. Being hundreds of miles long, it's understandable people would assume it sticks out like a sore thumb from space.

Yes, the Great Wall of China is very, very long. It's also built from rocks collected from all over the local landscape – in other words, ones that are usually the same color as the wall itself.

So unless China decides to give the wall a makeover and paint it hot pink, it's going to remain fairly hard to spot from space.

So what can astronauts see out the windows of the space station? Quite a bit, actually. Cities light up like spiderwebs at night, of course, but even during the day lots of stuff is visible. Bridges, dams, airports and major highways are among the structures seen by spacemen as they shoot across the sky, far above the pitiful, land-bound mortals on Earth.

7: Glass Is a Slow-moving Liquid

You may have lived for field trips as a kid, looking forward to a whole day of out-of-school fun and exploring. That is, until you got started on a tour of some musty building that seemed, well, boring. Not even the tour guide's explanation of how the glass in the wavy, uneven windowpanes has slowly flowed downward over time could keep your attention.

Liquid windowpanes? No.

Rather than the (magical-sounding) slow drip of centuries, the reason old glass windows aren't perfectly even and clear is because of how they were made. Until the early-mid 1800s, most window glass was made using a process called the crown method. The glass was blown, flattened, heated and spun, yielding a sheet that was relatively cheap to produce. It was also rippled and thicker in some places than in others.

In other words, the windows looked that way when they were installed, and they look that way now. No downhill liquid flow is involved. (And if you're really wondering: Glass is an amorphous solid. Learn more about it in "What makes glass transparent?")

6: Mother Birds Will Abandon Babies if You Touch Them

You're out in the yard and you see a distressing sight – a baby bird is floundering around on the ground, looking like it's desperate to get in the air, but it can't despite all its efforts. Suddenly, out of your peripherals, you spot a cat readying for a pounce. Sacre bleu! You rush over to scoop up the little bundle of feathers, take it into the house, and try to remember how to assemble a shoebox nest to serve as a habitat for your precious little find. You'll raise it yourself until it's ready to fly.

While this is wrong on several levels, it's not because you touched the bird.

Baby birds usually don't leave the nest until they're ready (or at least readyish) to fly. But, just like how well you drove during your very first driving lesson, they typically stink at flying at first. So needless to say, they suffer a few false starts and end up on the ground, whining like a teenager who wants the keys but hasn't completely got the hang of which is the gas and which is the brake.

But that doesn't mean the fledgling's parents aren't supervising their offspring. They're probably in a nearby tree, shuddering as their little dunce forgets all the lessons they taught it. And if you leave the baby bird alone, chances are they'll be there soon to smack it upside the head and tell it to pay more attention during the next round of flying lessons.

As for the scent issue – birds just don't smell too well. A few species are an exception, but chances are vastly greater that the little chirping ball of fluff won't suffer if you need to move it to the other side of the fence from where your dog plays. Plus, its parents have invested way too much time and energy raising it to just scoot off at the first opportunity, no matter how the little guy smells.

Nestlings Need a Little Helping Hand

If the baby bird you encounter is rather fuzzy or has no feathers at all, a little intervention is called for. Scoop it back up into its nest. Mom and Dad won't care (or likely even notice) if their offspring has a little eau de human on it. Read more in How to Rescue a Baby Bird.

5: Different Parts of Your Tongue Detect Different Tastes

Lots of people think different parts of the tongue are fine-tuned to detect different tastes. The tip of the tongue is where you get your cupcake on, the sides are where the salty taste really hits home, bitter's in the back, and in between is the sour zone. This "fact" was the prevailing notion for a very long time. It has persisted in spite of millions of kids in health class insisting that the wooden spoon just tastes like wooden spoon, no matter how they lick it.

More recently, however, we've found out that the whole zones theory was pretty much bologna. (That would be the umami talking. More about that in a sec.) It turns out people can sense different tastes all over their tongues. There are a few outliers, but for most people, them's the facts.

Then there's the fifth basic taste that doesn't get a lot of PR, and that's umami. Auguste Escoffier, the pimpest chef in 19th century France, concocted this fifth wheel in the palate party. Foodies swooned over it – it's been described as savory and meaty – but scientists stuck to the sweet/salty/bitter/sour taste tetrahedron.

Even though umami was a familiar taste in Japan, the "fifth taste" idea didn't get much traction there, either. That is until Kikunae Ikeda, a whiz-bang Japanese chemist, decided to get to the bottom of what umami was all about. He figured out the taste came from glutamic acid, and he called it the Japanese version of yummy.

No one at the time believed him, though, and it wasn't until the end of the 20th century that scientists decided to look into it. They realized Ikeda was right all along.

4: People Thought the World Was Flat Before Columbus

Christopher Columbus' crew had a lot to be worried about as they set sail. There was the possibility that they might wind up with scurvy or meander into a vengeful weather front, and of course there were all those warnings about where there be monsters.

But falling off the edge of the planet? Not so much. The idea that Columbus was endeavoring to attempt the unimaginable, defy all existing scientific precedent and become an international celebrity for not toppling off the world is false.

People have known since the learned and logic-laden age of the Greeks that they lived on a great, big globe. There were lots of obvious clues, like the way ships sailed over the horizon.

There were many objections to Columbus' plan to reach the East Indies via a somewhat novel route, but a tragic (and expensive) plunge into the abyss wasn't one of them. Most contentious were the logistics. Given the estimated (and not too shabby) size of the globe, there were steep odds his ships wouldn't successfully reach their intended destination. In the 1800s, the "knowledge" that our goofy, dark-ages ancestors had just up and forgotten the shape of the thing that they lived on started to circulate.

The Wrong Belief That Really Was

Flat Earth – not so much. But people really did believe that the Earth was at the center of the solar system. Physicists, mathematicians and astronomers thought up all kinds of complicated equations to explain why planets moved through the sky in a way that made no sense if they were orbiting Earth. Realizing that the planets orbited the sun solved that problem.

3: Deoxygenated Blood Is Blue

Everybody has veins snaking up and down their bodies, and those veins are blue. So it stands to reason that whatever magical and mysterious substance courses through those veins (all right, fine, it's just boring, old blood) is, as a matter of course, blue.

But no! Once your blood has stopped by the bank (your lungs) and picked up a withdrawal of cash monies (oxygen) it's flush with greenbacks (bright red blood). Once it's spent a night on the town (circulated through your body), it returns with a massive hangover (the blood has turned dark red) and it goes to curl up on the couch (take another pass through the heart).

Basically, the veins are blue thanks to a trick of the light, not the color of what's inside them.

2: Chameleons Change Color to Blend in With Surroundings

*Chameleons are one of the five coolest species in the world. That's a fact.**

They're wicked awesome for a number of reasons: their funny, little two-toed feet, their uber-mobile eye cups, their super curly tails and their other exciting physical embellishments. What's probably best about them, though, is their polychromatic flare. But all those changing colors, unlike what many people believe, usually don't have a thing to do with blending into their surroundings. It hinges on the particular species, of course, but they're usually pretty well camouflaged to begin with. If they need to visually merge into the background, they can just stick with their normal coloration.

Instead, chameleon color-changing is typically triggered by physical, physiological and emotional changes. If they're feeling fussy, say angry or afraid or combative, they'll change colors using their chromatophores. They'll also change colors as a way of communicating in various manners (insert romantic music here) and to pick a fight with a competitor. Light and temperature play a big part, too, in how these little fancy pantses look.

**Chameleons' rank as one of the five coolest species in the world is not, in fact, a fact. Although it is very, very likely.*

1: Humans Have Five Senses

We hear what you're saying. We see your point of view. We feel your pain. Also, you smell bad and possibly taste funny, the latter of which we don't intend to test.

But if you believe these are the only five ways you can detect information about your environment or alterations to your person, we're going to punch you in the face. There. Boom. You will feel it thanks to nociception, the ability to sense pain.

There are lots more, too, although the lists vary and the final number-of-senses tally is in great dispute. There are several boring ones that your body does without you knowing it. So let's skip those. More interesting is proprioception, which helps you pass the "close your eyes and touch your nose" test. Basically, it's what lets two parts of your body connect without visual confirmation. If you're (successfully) rubbing your eyes in disbelief, you used proprioception to do it. If you accidently smacked yourself in the forehead instead, you experienced a proprioception fail.

Apart from those, hunger and thirst can count according to some, as can feelings of hot and cold. Itch, interestingly, is apparently independent from both touch and pain. It's annoying on so many levels!

CHAPTER THREE

STILL HERE?

1. I'm sure you've heard the warning that if you dropped a penny from the top of the Empire State Building, it could kill someone on the street below.

This is simply false. It would not be able to gain enough velocity.

2. If your dog has ever been sprayed by a skunk, you probably washed them in a bath of tomato juice.

However, tomato juice does nothing to counteract the smell, and it is as ineffective as using any other strongly scented item.

3. Many ships and planes have ~mysteriously~ vanished in the Bermuda Triangle...

...but not significantly more than any other well-traveled waterways and oceans, as it turns out.

4. Has your mom ever told you to stock up on vitamin C during cold or flu season?

Well, tell your mom she was wrong, because vitamin C supplements have little to no effect on preventing or shortening a cold.

5. If you're Christian, you probably celebrate Christmas, aka Jesus' birthday.

Except it's not. The Bible references shepherds watching over their flocks during Jesus' birth, suggesting it was summertime (or at the very least not winter). There is no reference to any date — and certainly not December 25. In fact, no historical sources confirm that Christmas was celebrated then until 336 AD. It seems the date was chosen to appropriate the winter solstice — a pagan holiday — for Christian purposes, as it was around that time.

6. Also, Jesus would not have been white, nor is there any evidence that he had long hair.

There are very few references to Jesus' appearance in the Bible, but one suggests he had darker skin. Moreover, he was a Palestinian Jewish man and would've looked like one. Early art depicted him with short hair — the image of a long-haired Jesus started popping up in the fourth century and was influenced by art done of Greek and Roman gods.

7. You've probably heard the belief that dogs and cats age seven years for each human year...

For dogs, it's super dependent on size and breed, as different breeds have very different life expectancies. Also, for both dogs and cats, a lot of aging happens in the first two years — more than the "14 human years" the seven-year rule would suggest.

8. Someone has likely told you that the volcano in Yellowstone is overdue for an eruption.

If you're counting the average years between explosions, we still have 100,000 years to go — however, these numbers are largely meaningless, as volcanic eruptions are unpredictable.

Scientists are not even sure if there's enough magma for an eruption.

9. Another common belief is that worms become two worms when they're cut in half.

The half with the head may be able to grow back its tail and survive, but the half with the tail can't grow into a new worm and will die.

However, flatworms can regenerate into two worms when cut in half.

10. I'm sure you know the hit song "Don't Worry, Be Happy" by Bob Marley.

Except...he didn't sing the song. Bobby McFerrin did. In fact, it was written seven years after Marley's death.

Marley does have a song "Three Little Birds" with some similar words, themes, and phrases, likely causing the confusion.

11. Sticking with music, you've probably heard Phil Collins was inspired to write the song "In the Air Tonight" after witnessing someone drown and wanting to confront an onlooker who could've stopped it.

You may have heard the story, like me, from Eminem's song "Stan."

This is nothing more than an urban legend. Collins himself has stated that he wrote the song about his divorce.

12. Ah, the beautiful yellow sun...oh, wait a minute. It's not yellow at all.

It's actually white, which you can tell from space. It only appears yellow because we're looking at it through the atmosphere.

13. One of my favorite creepy facts is that people's hair and fingernails continue to grow after they die.

Which is why I was pretty saddened to find out it wasn't a fact at all! In actuality, skin around fingernails and hair follicles dry up and retract, which can make stubble and nails appear to have grown, even though they have not.

14. One of the coolest things about snakes is that their jaws can unhinge.

Except...they can't, actually. The lower bones of their jaws do not connect and are attached with a stretchy ligament that allows them to open their mouths super wide — but they aren't unhinging their jaws.

15. Did your mom ever tell you to eat carrots to improve your vision?

'Cause that's totally false! In fact, the idea was actively invented by the British government to spread misinformation that would hide the existence of their radar systems during World War II.

16. Cremating is a nice way to turn bodies into ashes, right?

Wrong! It leaves behind bone fragments, which are basically put into a blender until they fit in with the other ashes.

17. You may have been told you were a "left brain" person or a "right brain person."

However, abilities are not actually separated in this way. There are not "left brain dominant" or "right brain dominant" people, and most cognitive skills — like math, and even language (though dominant on the left) — rely on both sides of the brain.

18. You've probably heard that female praying mantises eat their male partner after mating.

This does happen, but not every time, and not with every species. In the species where this does happen, up to 28% of males are eaten by their partner.

19. You've probably heard of a "beer blanket" — aka the belief that you get warmer after drinking.

However, beer doesn't make you any warmer. You might feel like you're warmer — or you're at least distracted from the cold — but if anything, it's actually making you colder.

Drinking could mess with your body's reflexes to keep it warm.

20. What's also false? That alcohol kills brain cells.

However, it can damage the ends of neurons.

21. And that drinking liquor before beer prevents nausea/a hangover. That's right, folks: "Beer before liquor, never sicker; liquor before beer, in the clear" has no basis in

reality.

Your hangover will be just as bad either way!

22. Babies used to not be given any sort of pain-relieving drugs during surgery because people were taught that babies couldn't feel pain, and you may have been led to believe this, too.

But, uh...they definitely do. Now, there are ways to provide pain relief for infants, although some surgeries do proceed without it.

23. If you're babysitting or around any kids, their parents might've told you not to give them sugar because they get hyper.

However, sugar doesn't actually increase hyperactivity in kids!

24. You also might've heard parents talking about keeping their kids away from violent video games.

However, numerous studies have shown that violent video games don't make kids violent.

25. And finally, we've all heard about the G-spot...but there is no solid proof that the G-spot even exists.

Yup!

CHAPTER FOUR

NOW! TIME FOR SOME SARCASM

THESE FACTS ARE TRUE.

IRRELEVANT FOR A BOOK OF LIES, I KNOW,

BUT THAT'S WHY ITS A BOOK OF LIES AND I AM THE BEST LIAR.

1

The Supreme Court has its own private basketball court with an amazing nickname.

There's a basketball court on the top floor of the U.S. Supreme Court Building. Its nickname? You guessed it: "the highest court in the land." And for more trivia, here are the 100 Mind-Blowing Facts You've Never Heard Before.

2

Walmart has a lower acceptance rate than Harvard.

Harvard might be hard to get into with a 4.5 percent admittance rate, but try this on for size: only 2.6 percent of Walmart applicants are accepted. How 'bout them apples? Now, we realize that this comparison isn't exactly flawless, but you have to admit that it's a funny fact.

3

A football fan once dedicated his obit to insulting an NFL team.

True story: A lifetime Cleveland Browns fan and season ticket holder requested in his obituary for "six Cleveland Browns pallbearers" at his funeral. Why? "So the Browns can let him down one last time." Burn! And for more witty responses, These Are the Greatest Insults in History.

4

There is a technical name for the "fear of long words."

It's called "hippopotomonstrosesquippedaliophobia." And for more language facts, here are the 20 Words You Won't Believe Are in the Dictionary Now.

5

Hunting unicorns is legal in Michigan.

Lake Superior State University in Michigan offers a unicorn hunting license. Unsurprisingly, the "chief herald of the Unicorn Hunters" was once quoted saying: "The pursuit of the unicorn is a lonely quest." We wish them nothing but good luck!

6

Someone actually paid $10,000 for invisible artwork.

An art collector once paid $10,000 for a "non-visible" sculpture created by actor James Franco. The artwork was billed as an "endless tank of oxygen." Um, yeah... it's called air. We're breathing some now... for free!

7

There is an official ruling for how many Tootsie Pop licks it takes to get to the center.

It officially takes 364 licks to get to the center of a Tootsie Pop. Well, at least according to engineering students' scientific endeavor at Purdue University, who used a proprietary "licking machine" rather than a human tongue. And for more fun facts, sign up for our daily newsletter.

8

Cows moo with regional accents.

"In small populations such as herds you would encounter identifiable dialectical variations which are most affected by the immediate peer group," explains one UK professor in an article for BBC News. In other words: You can take the cow out of Jersey...

9

A U.S. town had a 3-year-old mayor.

In the small town of Dorset, Minnesota, where a new mayor is picked every two years by drawing names out of a hat, a 3 year old named Robert Tufts was elected mayor in 2015. His governing style: "Being nice and no poopy talk." In 2018, I think we can all agree that the world could use more Robert Tufts in higher office. And for more great trivia, here are 20 Crazy Facts That Will Blow Your Mind.

10

The Cookie Monster has a real name.

It's Sid. No, seriously.

11

China censored the word for "censorship."

I guess you can't be guilty of a crime if nobody can describe what it is! And for more fun info, don't miss the 125 Facts That Will Make You Feel Instantly Smarter.

12

Barry Manilow didn't write his hit song "I Write the Songs."

And before he recorded it, Barry didn't even think it was a particularly good song.

13

Vending machines are bigger threats to humanity than sharks.

You're twice as likely to be killed by a vending machine than a shark, according to the New England Aquarium. So when is Discovery Channel premiering their "Vending Machine Week?"

14

The blob of toothpaste that sits on your toothbrush has a name.

It's called a "nurdle."

15

Americans have a troubling understanding of computer code.

According to a 2014 study conducted by VoucherCloud and published by the Los Angeles Times, one in nine Americans—exactly 11 percent of the population—think HTML is actually a disease. Oof!

16

The Queen is a total wedding crasher!

If you invite the Queen of England to your wedding, even if you're not royalty, there's a chance she might show up anyway, as she did with one unsuspecting couple in Manchester in 2012.

17

You can hire scary clowns to terrify children.

You can hire a clown in Switzerland to stalk your kid and creepily smash a cake into their face on their birthday. Seriously. As if "nice" clowns weren't terrifying enough!

18

Flowers like Viagra.

Here's a funny fact: If you put some Viagra in a vase, it will make flowers stand up straight for a week beyond when they would normally wilt, according to one study conducted by Israeli and Australian researchers.

19

Terrorist instructions were once replaced with cupcakes.

Britain's Secret Intelligence Service once hacked an Al-Qaeda website and replaced the bomb instructions with a cupcake recipe.

20

There's an American town with a population of one.

Monowi, Nebraska, is the only town in the United States with an official population of one person. Yes, she owes taxes... To herself! She's in her 80s, and she's employed as the village's mayor, librarian, and bartender.

21

President Coolidge had a childish sense of humor.

Believe it or not, the 30th U.S. president thought it was hilarious to push the emergency buzzer on his desk and then hide when the Secret Service came running.

22

Some passengers go to insane lengths to avoid baggage fees.

In 2012, a man wore 60 shirts and nine pairs of jeans on an 11-and-a-half hour flight from China to Africa because he didn't want to pay the extra baggage fee. Though hilarious, I don't recommend it.

23

A bridge for squirrels exists.

A town in Washington has a treetop bridge over a busy road that's just big enough for squirrels. It's called the "Nutty Narrows Bridge." Admit it. That's undeniably funny.

24

One brogrammer had an unusual way of weaning himself off Facebook.

Maneesh Sethi, a computer programmer, hired a woman (at $8 an hour) to slap him in the face every time he tried checking Facebook during *working hours! Smartphone addiction is real people!*

25

Neil DeGrasse Tyson's surprising other career path isn't what you'd guess.

While he was in graduate school, astrophysicist Neil DeGrasse Tyson considered becoming a stripper to earn extra money, according to an interview with The University of North-South Whales. He visited a club and watched dancers perform to the song Great Balls of Fire. Tyson left immediately and became a math tutor instead. We're thrilled, of course.

26

One Norwegian town has a super ironic name.

There's a village in southern Norway actually named "Hell." And get this: every winter it freezes over!

27

Some silly constitutional amendments never happened.

A U.S. constitutional amendment was proposed in 1893 suggesting that the country be renamed "The United States of Earth." There was another failed amendment, a few years prior, that wanted to abolish the presidency and install a "Roman-style triumvirate." As if the United States needed any more comparisons to the doomed Roman Empire!

28

People aren't always praying for what you'd expect.

According to a 2014 survey by a Christian retailer LifeWay in Nashville, 7 percent of Christian Americans pray for a parking spot!

29

We have musical roads.

There's a highway in Lancaster, California, that plays the "William Tell Overture"—or the theme from "The Lone Ranger"—whenever cars drive over it at 55 mph. Yes, roads that sing!

30

We're more prepped for a zombie invasion than you probably knew.

The actual U.S. Centers for Disease Control and Prevention has a real website devoted to "zombie preparedness."

31

The brooding silence in the Twilight movies surprisingly adds up.

If you spliced them all together, there are exactly 26 minutes of quiet staring.

32

Lobsters communicate with their bladders.

Lobsters have bladders on either side of their heads, so they communicate by urinating at each other. If they want another lobster to know that they're happy or sad or angry or interested in a relationship, they say it with pee!

33

Dolly Parton lost a look-alike contest.

Dolly Parton once entered a celebrity look-alike contest, without revealing her true identity, at a club in San Francisco. She lost to a drag queen.

34

A man actually changed his name because he lost a bet.

After losing a drunken poker bet in 2009, a New Zealand man had his name legally changed to "Full Metal Havok More Sexy N Intelligent Than Spock And All The Superheroes Combined With Frostnova." It took five years, but the name was finally approved by the government. All 99 characters of his new name are on his passport.

35

Carrots just might turn you orange.

Want another funny fact? If you eat enough carrots—about three large carrots a day for several weeks—it increases the beta-carotene in your blood and could turn your skin orange.

36

People hate privacy policies (and reading the fine print in general).

It would take 76 workdays (if you work an eight-hour day) to read every online privacy policy you agree to in an average year.

37

Nabokov may be the real inventor of emojis.

Russian author Vladimir Nabokov came up with the idea for smiley emoticons in 1969.

38

High heels were originally for men.

When high-heel shoes first came into fashion in the 10th century, they were intended for men. It wasn't until the 18th century that more women wore high heels than men.

39

Latin America has flowers that look like lips.

There's a flower in the rainforests of Central and South America that resembles a puckering mouth covered in lipstick. It is called Psychotria Elata.

40

Cows don't like Willie Nelson.

Here's a funny fact for you: A dairy cow will produce up to 3 percent more milk when listening to music. But they don't like country music, especially Willie Nelson. They need something with a good beat.

Ok So, That's It Byee,

AND ONE LAST TIME...

LIES LIES LIES LIES LIES LIES LIES LIES
LIES LIES LIES LIES LIES LIES LIES LIES
LIES LIES LIES LIES LIES LIES LIES LIES
LIES LIES LIES LIES LIES LIES LIES LIES
LIES LIES LIES LIES LIES LIES LIES LIES
LIES LIES LIES LIES LIES LIES LIES LIES
LIES LIES LIES LIES LIES LIES LIES LIES
LIES LIES LIES LIES LIES LIES LIES LIES
LIES LIES LIES LIES LIES LIES LIES LIES
LIES LIES LIES LIES LIES LIES LIES LIES
LIES LIES LIES LIES LIES LIES LIES LIES
LIES LIES LIES LIES LIES LIES LIES LIES
LIES LIES LIES LIES LIES LIES LIES LIES
LIES LIES LIES LIES LIES LIES LIES LIES
LIES LIES LIES LIES LIES LIES LIES LIES
LIES LIES LIES LIES LIES LIES LIES LIES
LIES LIES LIES LIES LIES LIES LIES LIES
LIES LIES LIES LIES LIES LIES LIES LIES
LIES LIES LIES LIES LIES LIES LIES LIES
LIES LIES LIES LIES LIES LIES LIES LIES
LIES LIES LIES LIES LIES LIES LIES LIES
LIES LIES LIES LIES LIES LIES LIES LIES
LIES LIES LIES LIES LIES LIES LIES LIES
LIES LIES LIES LIES LIES LIES LIES LIES
LIES LIES LIES LIES LIES LIES LIES LIES
LIES LIES LIES LIES LIES LIES LIES LIES

*LIES LIES LIES LIES LIES LIES LIES LIES
LIES LIES LIES LIES LIES LIES LIES LIES
LIES LIES LIES LIES LIES LIES LIES LIES
LIES LIES LIES LIES LIES LIES LIES LIES
LIES LIES LIES LIES LIES LIES LIES LIES
LIES LIES LIES LIES LIES LIES LIES LIES
LIES LIES LIES LIES LIES LIES LIES LIES
LIES LIES LIES LIES LIES LIES LIES LIES
LIES LIES LIES LIES LIES LIES LIES LIES
LIES LIES LIES LIES LIES LIES LIES LIES
LIES LIES LIES LIES LIES LIES LIES LIES
LIES LIES LIES LIES LIES LIES LIES LIES
LIES LIES LIES LIES LIES LIES LIES LIES
LIES LIES LIES LIES LIES LIES LIES LIES
LIES LIES LIES LIES LIES LIES LIES LIES
LIES LIES LIES LIES LIES LIES LIES LIES
LIES LIES LIES LIES LIES LIES LIES LIES
LIES LIES LIES LIES LIES LIES LIES LIES
LIES LIES LIES LIES LIES LIES LIES LIES
LIES LIES LIES LIES LIES LIES LIES LIES
LIES LIES LIES LIES LIES LIES LIES LIES
LIES LIES LIES LIES LIES LIES LIES LIES
LIES LIES LIES LIES LIES LIES LIES LIES
LIES LIES LIES LIES LIES LIES LIES LIES
LIES LIES LIES LIES LIES LIES LIES LIES
LIES LIES LIES LIES LIES LIES LIES LIES
LIES LIES LIES LIES LIES LIES LIES LIES
LIES LIES LIES LIES LIES LIES LIES LIES
LIES LIES LIES LIES LIES LIES LIES LIES
LIES LIES LIES LIES LIES LIES LIES LIES
LIES LIES LIES LIES LIES LIES LIES LIES
LIES LIES LIES LIES LIES LIES LIES LIES
LIES LIES LIES LIES LIES LIES LIES LIES*

LIES LIES LIES LIES LIES LIES LIES LIES
LIES LIES LIES LIES LIES LIES LIES LIES
LIES LIES LIES LIES LIES LIES LIES LIES
LIES LIES LIES LIES LIES LIES LIES LIES
LIES LIES LIES LIES LIES LIES LIES LIES
LIES LIES LIES LIES LIES LIES LIES LIES
LIES LIES LIES LIES LIES LIES LIES LIES
LIES LIES LIES LIES LIES LIES LIES LIES
LIES LIES LIES LIES LIES LIES LIES LIES
LIES LIES LIES LIES LIES LIES LIES LIES
LIES LIES LIES LIES LIES LIES LIES LIES
LIES LIES LIES LIES LIES LIES LIES LIES
LIES LIES LIES LIES LIES LIES LIES LIES
LIES LIES LIES LIES LIES LIES LIES LIES
LIES LIES LIES LIES LIES LIES LIES LIES
LIES LIES LIES LIES LIES LIES LIES LIES
LIES LIES LIES LIES LIES LIES LIES LIES
LIES LIES LIES LIES LIES LIES LIES LIES
LIES LIES LIES LIES LIES LIES LIES LIES
LIES LIES LIES LIES LIES LIES LIES LIES
LIES LIES LIES LIES LIES LIES LIES LIES
LIES LIES LIES LIES LIES LIES LIES LIES
LIES LIES LIES LIES LIES LIES LIES LIES
LIES LIES LIES LIES LIES LIES LIES LIES
LIES LIES LIES LIES LIES LIES LIES LIES
LIES LIES LIES LIES LIES LIES LIES LIES
LIES LIES LIES LIES LIES LIES LIES LIES
LIES LIES LIES LIES LIES LIES LIES LIES
LIES LIES LIES LIES LIES LIES LIES LIES
LIES LIES LIES LIES LIES LIES LIES LIES
LIES LIES LIES LIES LIES LIES LIES LIES
LIES LIES LIES LIES LIES LIES LIES LIES
LIES LIES LIES LIES LIES LIES LIES LIES

LIES LIES LIES LIES LIES LIES LIES LIES
LIES LIES LIES LIES LIES LIES LIES LIES
LIES LIES LIES LIES LIES LIES LIES LIES
LIES LIES LIES LIES LIES LIES LIES LIES
LIES LIES LIES LIES LIES LIES LIES LIES
LIES LIES LIES LIES LIES LIES LIES LIES
LIES LIES LIES LIES LIES LIES LIES LIES
LIES LIES LIES LIES LIES LIES LIES LIES
LIES LIES LIES LIES LIES LIES LIES LIES
LIES LIES LIES LIES LIES LIES LIES LIES
LIES LIES LIES LIES LIES LIES LIES LIES
LIES LIES LIES LIES LIES LIES LIES LIES
LIES LIES LIES LIES LIES LIES LIES LIES
LIES LIES LIES LIES LIES LIES LIES LIES
LIES LIES LIES LIES LIES LIES LIES LIES
LIES LIES LIES LIES LIES LIES LIES LIES
LIES LIES LIES LIES LIES LIES LIES LIES
LIES LIES LIES LIES LIES LIES LIES LIES
LIES LIES LIES LIES LIES LIES LIES LIES
LIES LIES LIES LIES LIES LIES LIES LIES
LIES LIES LIES LIES LIES LIES LIES LIES
LIES LIES LIES LIES LIES LIES LIES LIES
LIES LIES LIES LIES LIES LIES LIES LIES
LIES LIES LIES LIES LIES LIES LIES LIES
LIES LIES LIES LIES LIES LIES LIES LIES
LIES LIES LIES LIES LIES LIES LIES LIES
LIES LIES LIES LIES LIES LIES LIES LIES
LIES LIES LIES LIES LIES LIES LIES LIES
LIES LIES LIES LIES LIES LIES LIES LIES
LIES LIES LIES LIES LIES LIES LIES LIES
LIES LIES LIES LIES LIES LIES LIES LIES
LIES LIES LIES LIES LIES LIES LIES LIES
LIES LIES LIES LIES LIES LIES LIES LIES

LIES LIES LIES LIES LIES LIES LIES LIES
LIES LIES LIES LIES LIES LIES LIES LIES
LIES LIES LIES LIES LIES LIES LIES LIES
LIES LIES LIES LIES LIES LIES LIES LIES
LIES LIES LIES LIES LIES LIES LIES LIES
LIES LIES LIES LIES LIES LIES LIES LIES
LIES LIES LIES LIES LIES LIES LIES LIES
LIES LIES LIES LIES LIES LIES LIES LIES
LIES LIES LIES LIES LIES LIES LIES LIES
LIES LIES LIES LIES LIES LIES LIES LIES
LIES LIES LIES LIES LIES LIES LIES LIES
LIES LIES LIES LIES LIES LIES LIES LIES
LIES LIES LIES LIES LIES LIES LIES LIES
LIES LIES LIES LIES LIES LIES LIES LIES
LIES LIES LIES LIES LIES LIES LIES LIES
LIES LIES LIES LIES LIES LIES LIES LIES
LIES LIES LIES LIES LIES LIES LIES LIES
LIES LIES LIES LIES LIES LIES LIES LIES
LIES LIES LIES LIES LIES LIES LIES LIES
LIES LIES LIES LIES LIES LIES LIES LIES
LIES LIES LIES LIES LIES LIES LIES LIES
LIES LIES LIES LIES LIES LIES LIES LIES
LIES LIES LIES LIES LIES LIES LIES LIES
LIES LIES LIES LIES LIES LIES LIES LIES
LIES LIES LIES LIES LIES LIES LIES LIES
LIES LIES LIES LIES LIES LIES LIES LIES
LIES LIES LIES LIES LIES LIES LIES LIES
LIES LIES LIES LIES LIES LIES LIES LIES
LIES LIES LIES LIES LIES LIES LIES LIES
LIES LIES LIES LIES LIES LIES LIES LIES
LIES LIES LIES LIES LIES LIES LIES LIES
LIES LIES LIES LIES LIES LIES LIES LIES
LIES LIES LIES LIES LIES LIES LIES LIES

*LIES LIES LIES LIES LIES LIES LIES LIES
LIES LIES LIES LIES LIES LIES LIES LIES
LIES LIES LIES LIES LIES LIES LIES LIES
LIES LIES LIES LIES LIES LIES LIES LIES
LIES LIES LIES LIES LIES LIES LIES LIES
LIES LIES LIES LIES LIES LIES LIES LIES
LIES LIES LIES LIES LIES LIES LIES LIES
LIES LIES LIES LIES LIES LIES LIES LIES
LIES LIES LIES LIES LIES LIES LIES LIES
LIES LIES LIES LIES LIES LIES LIES LIES
LIES LIES LIES LIES LIES LIES LIES LIES
LIES LIES LIES LIES LIES LIES LIES LIES
LIES LIES LIES LIES LIES LIES LIES LIES
LIES LIES LIES LIES LIES LIES LIES LIES
LIES LIES LIES LIES LIES LIES LIES LIES
LIES LIES LIES LIES LIES LIES LIES LIES
LIES LIES LIES LIES LIES LIES LIES LIES
LIES LIES LIES LIES LIES LIES LIES LIES
LIES LIES LIES LIES LIES LIES LIES LIES
LIES LIES LIES LIES LIES LIES LIES LIES
LIES LIES LIES LIES LIES LIES LIES LIES
LIES LIES LIES LIES LIES LIES LIES LIES
LIES LIES LIES LIES LIES LIES LIES LIES
LIES LIES LIES LIES LIES LIES LIES LIES
LIES LIES LIES LIES LIES LIES LIES LIES
LIES LIES LIES LIES LIES LIES LIES LIES
LIES LIES LIES LIES LIES LIES LIES LIES
LIES LIES LIES LIES LIES LIES LIES LIES
LIES LIES LIES LIES LIES LIES LIES LIES
LIES LIES LIES LIES LIES LIES LIES LIES
LIES...*

I JUST LOVE THIS WORD

9 798887 496795

Printed by Libri Plureos GmbH in Hamburg,
Germany